A DK PUBLISHING BOOK

Managing Editor Bridget Gibbs
Senior Designer Claire Jones
Designer Lisa Hollis
DTP Designer Kim Browne
Production Katy Holmes
Photography Dave King
US Editor Kristin Ward

First American Edition, 1997
2 4 6 8 10 9 7 5 3 1

Published in the United States by DK Publishing, Inc.
95 Madison Avenue, New York, New York 10016

Visit us on the World Wide Web at http://www.dk.com

Published in Great Britain by Dorling Kindersley Limited.

ISBN 0-7894-2222-0

Color reproduction by G.R.B. Graphica, Verona
Printed in Singapore by Tien Wah Press (Pte) Ltd

Acknowledgments
DK would like to thank the following manufacturers for permission to photograph copyright material:
Ty Inc. for "Freddie" the frog
The Manhattan Toy Company Ltd. for "Antique Rabbit"
Folkmanis Inc. for "Furry Folk" hen puppet

DK would like to thank Barbara Owen, Vera Jones, Dave King,
and Steve Gorton for their help in producing this book.

Where Is P.B. Bear?

LEE DAVIS

Can you find me on each page?

DK PUBLISHING, INC.

P.B. Bear plays hide-and-seek.
While he hides you must not peek.

Look around.
Where can he be?

Turn the page
and you will see.

Look in the hall.
Where can he be?

Turn the page and you will see.

Look in the kitchen. Where can he be?

Turn the page
and you will see.

Look in the bedroom.
Where can he be?

Turn the page and you will see.

Look in the playroom. Where can he be?

Turn the page and you will see.

Look by the door. Where can he be?

Turn the page and you will see.

Take one last look.
Where can he be?

Turn the page and you will see.